MW01698226

Creating Community

Transforming Lives through Mutual Support

by Barbara Howard

William V. D'Antonio

© 2003 by Buena Vista, Inc.
Printed in the United States of America

All rights reserved. No part of this book may be reproduced or transmitted in any form or by any means, electronic or mechanical, including photocopying, recording, or any information storage and retrieval system, without the written permission of the publisher.

Scripture excerpts taken from the *New American Bible* © 1991, 1986, 1970 Confraternity of Christian Doctrine, Washington, D.C.

Living the Good News
a division of the Morehouse Group
Editorial Offices
600 Grant St., Suite 400
James R. Creasey, Publisher

Published in cooperation with Buena Vista, Inc.
P.O. Box 745475
Arvada, CO 80006
bv@buenavista.org
www.buenavista.org
303-477-0180

Originally published by Buena Vista Inc. as *Ubi Caritas,* 1996

Prayers and meditations from:
Prayers for a New World Order, by Betsy Clark, SSJ
© 1995 by Paulist Press
Reprinted with permission from Paulist Press, Mahwah, NJ

Radical Grace: Daily Reflections, by Richard Rohr
© 1993 by Richard Rohr and John Bookser Feister
Reprinted with permission from St. Anthony Messenger Press, Cincinnati, OH

Rituals and Icebreakers: Practical Tools for Forming Community, by Kathleen O'Connell Chesto Reprinted with permission from Sheed and Ward. Now published by Ligouri Press, Ligouri, MO, 1999.

ISBN 1-931960-05-4

Contents

Foreword

Since 1987, Buena Vista has been networking small Christian communities and offering support and resources for forming and nurturing SCCs.

Buena Vista members believe that being Christian and being church are synonymous. They also believe that church and community are synonymous. Therefore, it follows that being a Christian means being in community. Or, stated another way, living the Christian life outside of community is impossible. For most of us, the experience of church is within the parish or congregation, mainly in a large group on Sunday morning. The recent reemergence of small communities—within parishes and through religious congregations—has brought renewal, hope and a way to break down the large size of most congregations making community and church more relevant.

The Christian church at its roots is about small groups gathering in homes to remember Jesus and to be sent into the world to proclaim the love of God. These activities from our deepest tradition are what it means to be church. The booklets in this series are designed to help groups focus on becoming church.

As a grassroots, Catholic organization, Buena Vista has taken a biblical version of church and applied it to the life of small communities. The vision consists of four dimensions: *koinonoia*—mutuality, love and care within the community; *diakonia*—service and striving for justice within and outside of the community; *leitourgia*—praying and sacramentalizing the life of the community; and *kerygma*—being grounded in the Christian story. Our mission statement affirms four fundamental essentials of church and of SCCs: mutuality/community, service/justice, prayer/ritual and scripture/gospel-based witness. With this printing of the small community resource booklets, Buena Vista updates the first four volumes in our series designed to create conversation within and among SCCs.

Through these resources for small communities, we offer an opportunity for new and experienced groups to focus on essential activities of small Christian community life. Each booklet may be used independently or in succession with the other volumes. Each was written by a team of experienced small community practitioners who draw on their connection with the Buena Vista network of small Christian communities and years of ministry in facilitation and training for small Christian community development.

Creating Community helps your SCC to look at what shapes its identity and interior life, and provides background about the need for community as we become church. *Living Scripture* weaves the universal story of salvation into the small group experience, focusing on the deep meaning it gives to our lives as individuals and as a community. It explores our relationship as individuals and communities to the Great Stories of God's salvation, providing guidance for reflection on scripture and its use in small Christian communities. *Designing Ritual* helps small communities to understand the role of ritual prayer in expressing the sacredness of life. It contains practical steps for designing rituals to use in your own small Christian community. *Seeking Justice* addresses the public life of faith—why and how our SCCs are called to respond to scripture by making a difference in the greater community—with steps for community discernment and models for action.

The booklets in the series can be used in any order. They are appropriate for deepening the experience of small communities that have been meeting for years, or as an introduction to small Christian community for new groups.

With gratitude to the original authors, former Buena Vista national coordinator Barb Darling, recent reviewers, and our editors at Living the Good News, we offer these updated volumes for use by your small Christian communities. Each booklet contains useful information about the topic it addresses in the context of six easy-to-use small community sessions. We hope the dialogue within and among groups will be fruitful and challenging, leading to more effective mission. We look forward to hearing your reflections about the essentials of community on which your group chooses to focus, and about their reality in the experience of your SCC, and in the network of SCCs that our membership comprises. Enjoy one another as you deepen your faith and engage in discovery about your relationship with God in community.

Amy Sheber Howard
Buena Vista Executive Director
National Coordinator

Introduction

Community, rightly understood, is a nourishing environment in which we grow to become the unique people God created us to be. Community is or can be an effective corrective to the individualism so prevalent in our society. Community can become the forum for our stories of joy and struggle. At its best, community is a gift from God, a gift that needs to be cultivated and developed in order for its true value to permeate and enrich the church and the world. For at its best, community becomes the vehicle by which relationships of love and caring are developed.

This volume in the essentials series, originally titled *Ubi Caritas* (where there is love and caring for others, there is God), concentrates on that part of being church that connects individuals to one another through mutuality and intimacy beyond the family. In those human connections, when community begins to happen, we feel and know that something greater than just the sum of the parts is molding us into more than we are.

The six sessions of this resource explore the sociological phenomenon of the human need for community and the distinctive nature of small Christian community. New small communities can use this series as a means of formation and inspiration. Existing communities will find both resonance and challenge in the sessions of this series.

Session One
Why Community?

Scripture
Facilitator asks someone who has planned ahead to read the scripture aloud:

> There was a scholar of the law who stood up to test him and said, "Teacher, what must I do to inherit eternal life?" Jesus said to him, "What is written in the law? How do you read it?" He said in reply, "You shall love the Lord, your God, with all your heart, with all your being, with all your strength, and with all your mind, and your neighbor as yourself." He replied to him, "You have answered correctly; do this and you will live."
>
> *—Luke 10:25-28*

Focus Question
In groups of two, take five minutes to prepare for the gathering by discussing:

❍ How has your concept of neighbor changed during the past ten years?

Commentary
Take turns reading the following commentary aloud, with a new reader for each paragraph:

"Love your neighbor as you love yourself." That's easy, if...as...and when... There are a number of ideas to ponder in the great commandment that Jesus gave us. Jesus did not say that we should love our neighbor more than or less than we love ourselves, only just as much as we love ourselves. Frankly, if we are honest, there are times when we don't love ourselves much. Jesus seems to be acknowledging how difficult it is to love our neighbor even as he avoids any demand for self-sacrificing love. At the same time, the great commandment binds us necessarily to our neighbor, and thus provides an apparently easy answer to the question, "Why community?" But does it?

In one way or another we live out our lives in community, or more likely in today's world, in an interlocking web of communities. While Jesus' great commandment may urge us to seek out our neighbor throughout the vast web, one does not need much time for reflection to recognize how difficult, even at times unpleasant, a challenge that commandment is. Perhaps Richard Rohr's story about stone houses will help our reflection.

Stone Houses

This little old black African man and I prayed together after [I had preached] a long session. He prayed with such tenderness. He said, "O Lord, help us never to move into stone houses." And everybody echoed, "Yes, Lord. Yes, Lord."

Afterward I asked the missionaries what he had meant. "Well," a priest said, "look at the villages. They're all doorless thatch huts. And so long as you live a simple life in a thatch hut with no doors, you don't know where your family ends and where the next family begins. You move in and out of one another's lives, and it's all really one family. And there's no possessing; there's no mine and thine; it's ours. It's a world of community."

"Once the first stone hut is built in a village," the missionary continued, "very quickly a door and locks are put on it. Immediately the world of mine and thine is created. The entire social world view, the entire understanding of self, changes." (from *Radical Grace: Daily Meditations* by Richard Rohr)

We've got to realize the world of stone huts is the only world you and I have ever known. We've paid a price for that inheritance. We can't reverse it. We're not going to live in thatch huts, and I'm not here to say we should. But, we should know what we've given up by the so-called technological advances of a sophisticated society.

As we reflect on the many communities of which we are a part, it's important to understand how they function in our lives. Concentration on the following questions may help us analyze how these communities view neighbor. How do physical barriers reflect the social and psychological barriers that often restrict our understanding of neighbor? How important to the idea of community is the adjective that modifies the word? Does it help if we try to compare communities that are open with those that are closed? Can a Christian community be a closed community?

Sharing Questions

Let each person who wishes respond to the questions below before anyone speaks a second time, then let open conversation begin:

- ❍ What brought me to the SCC of which I am now a member?
- ❍ What tension(s) do I experience between individualism and communal life?

❍ How do I perceive the difference between a support group and a small Christian community?

Action

Take a drive around your neighborhood this week.

❍ How many yards are surrounded by tall wooden "privacy" fences?
❍ How many homes have front porches with chairs or other inviting settings?

Introduce yourself to a neighbor with whom you've never spoken.

Shared Prayer

Facilitator invites group members to quiet themselves for prayer, then reads this prayer aloud:

> Loving God, we hold in prayer before you all the concerns of our hearts and our lives. As a community we now share our prayers of thankfulness and of petition.

At this time, members share intentions for the community and personal intentions.

Closing Prayer

God of Huts

God of Huts, thanks and praise to you for
your presence and activity in the life of
our community.
Help our stone houses and hard hearts to
become open doors.
May we receive each other and strangers
here in your name. Amen.

—Rick Connor

Session Two

Community: Who's In and Who's Out?

Scripture

Facilitator asks someone who has prepared ahead to read the scripture aloud:

> There is neither Jew nor Greek, there is neither slave nor free person, there is not male and female; for you are all one in Christ Jesus.
>
> —*Galatians 3:28*

Focus Question

In groups of two, take five minutes to prepare for the session by discussing:

- When you meet a new person, how reliable is your "first impression" of her or him? Why?

Commentary

Take turns reading the following commentary aloud, with a new reader for each paragraph:

The following reflection was submitted unsigned in the general comments section of a broad-based survey conducted by a large, suburban parish:

"One thing which has been bothering me for some time is the concept of small Church communities. The drive to form a multitude of small Church communities has been growing for several years and seems to have significant rewards to those parishioners who are included. Tremendous personal enrichment is possible through a small community but I am very concerned about the net effect on society as well as our total Church community.

"In our country today, I see a major fragmentation of what I was raised to believe was a wonderful concept. Our country represented welcome to the stranger and shared common goals of freedom and independence. Now, through the divisiveness of a multitude of small interest groups, the American heritage is being chopped up into different cultural, racial, social, political and other special interest groups and the good of the whole is no longer a priority.

"We have the Religious Right, the Moral Majority, the African Americans, the Environmentalists, the Pro-Choicers and on and on. All these groups believe that they have the answers and that everyone should buy into their beliefs and anyone who doesn't is wrong. All their activities are directed toward their own narrow goals, without serious consideration of the consequences to the whole society.

"The same thing happens as the church slowly divides into small Church communities. Theoretically, all the small communities should share the same goal of uniting people to further God's Kingdom, but as the special interest groups break off into small communities, they begin to lose touch with the other groups. For example, our parish has small communities for seniors, singles, youth, gays, middle-aged couples and others, but they are losing contact with each other. We have a small community which very rudely ostracized one member whom they learned was gay. The person ended up leaving the group and joining the only all-gay community which seemingly has little contact with other small communities.

"Yes, I see value in the small Church community system, but I am disturbed by the problems it creates. I have been a member of the parish for ten years and in that time I have seen some of the effects of this fragmentation. I do not have a solution to this problem. It is certain that the breakdown will continue, and I am sad about that."

"Clearly the author has not only strong feelings regarding his/her perception of the current social context of the United States, but also concerns regarding the development of small Christian communities in the parish."

Whether one agrees or disagrees with the author's overall impressions, the comments are not easily dismissed. To be *Christian communities* our mandate is not to be an in-group but rather to be inclusive, to recognize those outside our group as our brother and our sister. The sociological construction of an in-group is "any group one belongs to and identifies with as being somehow special. Correspondingly, the in-group tends to regard the out-group (any alternative group that one does not belong to or identify with) as less worthy, and may even view it with hostility" (Robertson, *Sociology,* 173).

The in-group often labels all those outside of its own norms and mores as "other." This labeling has been a human experience since people first gathered in social groupings. Jesus upset the notion of in-group. He called all to the reign of God. "The call of Jesus cuts through all the castes, clean and unclean; male and female; zealots and tax collectors. He called Mary Magdalene 'from whom seven demons had gone out,' and Joanna, 'a member of the official household of Herod Antipas.' The call to discipleship is the great leveler" (Rademacher, *Lay Ministry,* 22).

As we consider community it is important to understand that the idea of community has multiple dimensions. In the sociological and psychological literature these dimensions embrace territorial, dependency and relational aspects. In MacIver's classic definition, the "mark of a community is that one's life may be lived within it, that all one's social relationships may be found in it" (MacIver, *Society: Its Structure and Changes,* 9).

Ronald Warren in *The Community in America* expanded on MacIver as follows:

> "Psychologically, it implies shared interests, characteristics, or association...Geographically, community denotes a specific area where people are clustered. Sociologically, the term combines these two connotations. It relates to the shared interests and behavior patterns which people have by virtue of their common locality."

Other writers have noted how communities have changed as the division of labor in society has changed, radically altering degrees of autonomy and dependency. The changes of the past 100 years have greatly disrupted ethnic/religious closed communities, but have clearly not done away with them. Common interests, shared values, geographic location, varying levels of interdependency: all help shape our idea of community. But this idea is challenged by the growth of special interest groups or organizations epitomized by the giant business and government bureaucracies, and a bureaucratic church seeking to propound universal values.

Mutual support is a core element in SCC life and inclusiveness is a core element in church life. If we find our community more interested in making sure that those we allow into our community think, act and look like we do, we may be missing the great gift of others whom God would like to send to broaden, enrich and perhaps challenge our small church. Clearly numbers are a consideration in the make-up of small Christian community. Membership in an SCC is limited by the physical space in which it gathers. But if a community has the physical space and still hesitates to add new people it may be important to spend time reflecting on the issue of inclusiveness.

Sharing Questions

Let each person who wishes respond to the questions below before anyone speaks a second time, then let open conversation begin:

- ❍ What rings true to you in the descriptions we have just heard of community, and small Christian community in particular?
- ❍ What from the above reading might our community need to think about further?
- ❍ How is it that closed Christian communities ("in-groups") persist in the face of the powerful scriptural injunction of Galatians 3:28?
- ❍ What makes it difficult to be inclusive?

❍ When was the last time I/we reached out to someone different from myself/ourselves?

Action

Fr. Jose Marins, et al, in the book *The Church from the Roots: Basic Ecclesial Communities,* urges that we think of small Christian communities in the following terms, differentiating communities from other groups:

Community	Group
The community is a global response to the totality of life, integrating all the fundamental social dimensions of the human being (family, education, health, economy, politics, leisure, religion) into the pursuit of a common goal.	The group is specialized, responding to one particular problem or aspect of life.
Pluralistic, bringing together persons of different ages, social standing, gender, culture and race, conscientization, religious practice, etc. Nevertheless, the members of the community must also work toward the same goals; they are people with common interests.	Usually homogenous, consisting of people more or less the same age, sex and specialization and tending toward uniformity—first of ideas, and afterwards of language, symbol and even dress.

Community	Group
Establishes relationships of a communal nature which are open-ended, thus avoiding the temptation to lapse into a ghetto mentality or to form elitist groups. In the community there is intimacy, friendship and an openness towards all.	Generally goes beyond friendships, tending towards intimacy. The group tends to equalize the intimacy, including everyone in the same rhythm.

Sharing Questions

Spend some time analyzing your community according to Marins' distinctions.

Either in conversation with another community member or by yourself, ask and attempt to answer the following questions:

- ❍ In what ways does this community have goals like those described by Marins as belonging to communities?
- ❍ In what ways are we more like other groups?
- ❍ Does our membership look more like what Marins describes as a community or a group?
- ❍ Where might our community be called to diversity in membership?
- ❍ Are there ways in which the relationships of our community could be more open?

Shared Prayer

Facilitator invites group members to quiet themselves for prayer, then reads this prayer aloud:

> Loving God, we hold in prayer before you all the concerns of our hearts and our lives. Help us to keep in mind all those who are marginalized by society, the modern day lepers, tax collectors and prostitutes. Open our eyes so that we may see beyond differences to the human face of God. As a community we now share our prayers of thankfulness and of petition.

At this time, members share intentions for the community and personal intentions.

Closing Prayer

In Your Image

Loving God, we gather to praise and thank
you for the unique expression of the Divine
that each one of us reflects.
We recognize in each other your image.
We acknowledge that at times we fail to see
and love that which you see and love.
Open our hearts and clear our minds that we
might know you as you know each of us.
In your mercy, hear our prayer. Grant us new
insight. *Amen.*

(from *Prayers For A New World Order*
by Betsy Clark, SSJ)

Session Three

How Does Our Community Function?

Scripture

Facilitator asks someone who has prepared ahead to read the scripture aloud:

> But Jesus summoned them and said, "You know that the rulers of the Gentiles lord it over them, and the great ones make their authority over them felt. It shall not be so among you. Rather, whoever wishes to be great among you shall be your servant; whoever wishes to be first among you shall be your slave. Just so, the Son of Man did not come to be served but to serve and to give his life as a ransom for many."
>
> —*Matthew 20:25-28*

Focus Question

In groups of two, take five minutes to prepare for the session by discussing:

- Have you ever been "in charge" of something or someone? What was the hardest thing about being "in charge"?

Commentary

Take turns reading the following commentary aloud, with a new reader for each paragraph:

So often in the past when we spoke about church we immediately envisioned either our local parish church building or a pyramidal, organizational structure that depicted (in descending levels) God, the pope, bishops, priests, religious and, at the bottom, laity. According to Fr. Raymond Brown, noted Scripture scholar and author of *The Churches the Apostles Left Behind*, much of that hierarchical understanding of church is founded in the strong emphasis put on the Gospel of Matthew. The gospel drew heavily on rabbinical models of authority which had clear laws and specific understanding of the role of authority. "[Matthew] is the only gospel that uses the word 'church.' Of all the gospels it was best suited to the manifold needs of the later church, the most cited by the church fathers, the most used in liturgy, and the most serviceable for catechetics" (Brown, 123). The church of Matthew, probably composed of Jewish Christians with a contingent of Gentile Christians, however, was only one model of the early churches described in the New Testament.

In his encyclical *Divino Afflante Spiritu*, Pope Pius XII encouraged serious biblical studies. The wealth of biblical scholarship undertaken in the past half-century has resulted in an understanding of an early church with a variety of structures and leadership styles. Brown suggests that New Testament churches had quite diverse emphases in their community life. While one style cannot represent the whole of the church, none should be thought inconsequential to the life of the whole church. Vatican II called us to a vision of Church as the People of God. That vision has given birth to new ministries, to new movements within the church and to new styles of leadership. While that vision cannot encompass the whole understanding of church, it is one that gives fullness to an until-recently neglected experience of the early church.

Small Christian communities are an expression of church that reaches into our communal history. We are reclaiming a style of church based on a gathering of people called by baptism to the mission of Jesus. The manner in which the church gathers is important, but not as important as the vision of the church as the people of God. "That vision begins with the inner conviction that the church was born not only from the death and resurrection of Christ, but also from the Holy Spirit on the day of Pentecost. In this new vision the reality of God's people is primary, the form of its organization and structure is secondary" (Rademacher, 123).

While it is necessary for an SCC to develop and maintain a structure that allows the community to function—concerning location, frequency and length of meetings, materials to be used for reflection and sharing, facilitation of meetings, good listening/communication skills—prominence should be given to the people gathered. The challenge to SCC members, in keeping with their baptismal call, is to honor one another's experience, welcome the stranger, acknowledge and resolve/manage conflict, learn forgiveness, work at honest communication and value the common good.

The leadership employed in a small Christian community needs to be one of facilitating the participation of all members rather than one of correct order and/or literal interpretation. As we grow more comfortable in this new/old style of church, however, it is important that we remember that other styles of church also exist just as they did in the early church. It is not as critical for us to convince others of the authenticity of the SCC style of church as it is for us to be the people of God together. "Sects can pride themselves on a purism that drives out all who do not meet an ideal, but a church has to show patience and mercy" (Brown, 133).

Sharing

Members of the community take turns reading the following.

Small Christian Community Agreement

We will make attendance at meetings a priority. A large part of the success of a small community depends on the commitment of its members to be at every meeting except for emergencies.

We agree to share ourselves. Personal sharing is the basis for building and maintaining our relationships. We will be honest and express our feelings about life and faith. The SCC is a place where we can be accepted for who we are.

We will listen to each other with patience and try to be understanding and appreciative of others' feelings. We will not give unsolicited advice or counsel.

We will respect the viewpoints and opinions of each individual. Differences of opinion and diversity of giftedness enhance our group.

We will support each other in appropriate ways. Encouragement and affirmation are important in our relationships. Physical, emotional and spiritual support will be given as needs are made known.

We agree to work through conflicts as they arise. We recognize that unexpressed negative feelings can be destructive. Instead of using ridicule and attack, we will be honest about how a member's behavior affects us and look at ways to improve the situation and relationship. We will look at conflict as an opportunity for the growth of the SCC.

We agree to keep what is said at our meetings confidential. When we share openly and honestly we expect that it will not leave the group.

Have each member of the community share one point they believe to be a strength in the community. After all have shared a strength, each shares a point that they believe needs further growth. (Don't worry if members have differing views over the community's perceived strengths and areas for growth. Admitting differences of opinion makes new directions possible.)

Action

If your community has been able to identify one or more areas for growth within the community, plan for specific ways in which those areas can be addressed. Share with one another at your next meeting ways that you will work on a particular growth area.

Shared Prayer

Facilitator invites group members to quiet themselves for prayer, then reads this prayer aloud:

> Loving God, we hold in prayer before you all the concerns of our hearts and our lives. As a community we now share our prayers of thankfulness and of petition.

At this time, members share intentions for the community and personal intentions.

Closing Prayer

New World Order

Today bursts forth with dawn and
  I stand before You in awe.
Today is a whole new day begging
  for your touch.
Give us new insight.
Help us to recognize that "order"
  does not mean "control."
Rather, it could mean we learn
  new ways to find each other.
To gaze into each other's eyes
  and see there the beauty
  of a sister or a brother.
  Amen.

(adapted from *Prayers For A New World Order* by Betsy Clark, SSJ)

Session Four
Our Common Priesthood

Scripture
Facilitator asks someone who has prepared ahead to read the scripture aloud:

> Above all, let your love for one another be intense, because love covers a multitude of sins. Be hospitable to one another without complaining. As each has received a gift, use it to serve one another as good stewards of God's varied grace. Whoever preaches, let it be with the words of God; whoever serves, let it be with the strength that God supplies, so that in all things God may be glorified through Jesus Christ, to whom belong glory and dominion forever and ever. Amen.
>
> *—1 Peter 4:8-11*

Focus Question
In groups of two, take five minutes to prepare for the session by discussing:

❍ What is your special talent?

Commentary
Take turns reading the following commentary aloud, with a new reader for each paragraph:

One of the great rediscoveries and conversely one of the great challenges of the Second Vatican Council was acknowledgment of the common priesthood of the faithful. By virtue of our Baptism into the Christian community each of us is commissioned to share in the priestly, prophetic and kingly mission of Jesus Christ. In the past we presumed that mission or ministry was set aside for those formally called to orders or to religious life. The laity were to perform acts of charity as encouraged or directed by our bishops or pastors. Vatican II ended the long process which had narrowed the concept of shared ministry present in the early church but made rigid and formalized in succeeding centuries. Returning to a New Testament understanding of Baptism and the gifts of the Spirit opened the way for recognition of a wider spectrum of ministries arising from the People of God.

Participation in a small Christian community helps us in a special way to discern and implement our unique gifts for ministry. Within the SCC we are affirmed and challenged by those we love and trust. When we first gather, often as a group of strangers, we may be fearful and reluctant to talk but as we become more comfortable with one another it is easier to share our stories. In our storytelling we learn how to listen to one another and how to sense the Spirit's movement in our own and in one another's lives. We encourage and support one another and we begin to appreciate and validate one another's gifts. Those gifts are often first used at the service of the small Christian community.

There are internal ministries that must be performed if the community is to have life. Everyone in the community has something to offer for the common good of the whole community. "The distinctive insight of the base communities is to see these tasks as ministries. There needs to be someone to organize a meeting, someone to offer hospitality, someone to plan an agenda, someone to read from the Bible, someone to say a prayer, someone to lead the singing, someone to look after the purse, someone to coordinate the community with other communities or with the parish, someone for other members to turn to for a listening ear, and so on" (Hebblethwaite, *Base Communities*, 118).

Ministry is vital to the internal life of the community; however, it is not confined within the community. Ministry moves out, supported and nurtured by the community, into the broader areas of family, parish, marketplace and culture. The priestly, prophetic and kingly nature of the Christian mission is to take our experience of God's love to all areas of our life. But ministry is not cold and sterile with exact clarity of definition and precise outcomes. Our call is to be in conversation with life as we encounter it. That requires an openness on our part to the ministries we perform in our small communities and to the ministry to which the Spirit calls us in the broader areas of our lives.

"Ministry, insofar as it is part of a truly human process, requires a constant dialogue. It means that ministers are dialogical persons who are disposed to be changed by the thing or the person with whom they are in dialogue. To be truly dialogic means to die to our own opinions and judgments so that our person becomes a hospitable place, welcoming the strangers, including...creation, into our lives on their own terms. The ministers who have a reverence for the holiness of the human will see reality not as something to be controlled or manipulated, but as a mystery... Christian ministers never really know what effects their words, actions, or the sacrament of their presence will have. All relationships are mystery and ministry is par excellence a relationship of mystery" (Rademacher, 134-135).

Sharing Questions

Let each person who wishes respond to the questions before anyone speaks a second time, then let open conversation begin:

- How am I gifted for ministry?
- How has ministry changed me?
- What do I find uncomfortable about ministry?
- What might be the importance for us, as a community, in having a shared ministry?

Action

Do one or more of the following actions either as a group at this session or individually in the coming week:

- Review the ministries being done by each person within your community.
- List the responsibilities that our baptismal call urges upon us in the larger communities in which we live.
- Consider as a community exploring the public life of ministry using the SCC booklet *Seeking Justice: Participating in the Public Life of Faith* (Living the Good News/Buena Vista).

Shared Prayer

Facilitator invites group members to quiet themselves for prayer, then reads this prayer aloud:

> Loving God, we hold in prayer before you all the concerns of our hearts and our lives. As a community we now share our prayers of thankfulness and of petition.

At this time, members share intentions for the community and personal intentions.

Closing Prayer

Prayer for Wisdom

Tender, compassionate One, hear my prayer for wisdom,
As I discern your way for me.
In this age of advanced technology and sophisticated
answers to questions of life and death, I feel overwhelmed.
I listen to your voice within me. Speak now.
Draw me close to you that I might hear your words.
What is it you ask of me?
As I make this decision, help me to recognize the value of my own gifts.
Clarify with me the pros and cons of this situation.
Give me a sense of true conviction.
Enlighten my doubts and strengthen my resolve so I will
make a decision pleasing to you, for the good
of my brothers and sisters and all of creation.

(from *Prayers for a New World Order*
by Betsy Clark, SSJ)

Session Five

CONNECTING WITH OTHER COMMUNITIES

Scripture

Facilitator asks someone who has prepared ahead to read the scripture aloud:

> He came and preached peace to you who were far off and peace to those who were near, for through him we all have access in one Spirit to the Father.
>
> So then you are no longer strangers and sojourners, but you are fellow citizens with the holy ones and members of the household of God, built upon the foundation of the apostles and prophets with Christ Jesus himself as the capstone. Through him the whole structure is held together and grows into a temple sacred in the Lord; in him you also are being built together into a dwelling place of God in the Spirit.
>
> —*Ephesians 2:17-22*

Focus Question

In groups of two, take five minutes to prepare for the session through discussion of the following question:

❍ Recall a time when you were alone in a new situation: a new job, new member of a class, new to a neighborhood, etc. What helped you feel like you belonged?

Commentary

Take turns reading the following commentary aloud, with a new reader for each paragraph:

More and more often people remark "what a small world!" The declaration is in response to a variety of events, such as discovering that your new next-door neighbor and your brother-in-law grew up in the same neighborhood in a distant city. They even had some mutual friends! "What a small world" remarks are elicited for a variety of reasons, but almost always because of a human, experiential connection between two or more people. "You visited the Potter's House in Washington, D.C.? We did too. When were you there?" These types of encounters help us to make connections, and to share, examine and validate our experience.

We know the value when we connect *within* our small Christian community. It is also vital for small Christian communities not to isolate themselves but to connect with other communities to share information, experience and the life of the Body of Christ. We gain strength, imagination and hope from our contact with one another. In a way this is a difficult concept especially for parish-based communities whose primary affiliation is the parish. It may seem unnecessary for small Christian communities to meet with one another since the majority of SCC members are involved in parish activities beyond their SCC membership. But it is precisely when SCCs meet with one another that they share and deepen the style of church that calls its members to full participation as a Christian community. It is important that parish-based communities—

not just their leaders—come together to share their experience one on one. It is also important that parishes provide the opportunity for SCCs meeting within the parish to meet with SCCs in other parishes.

The early church grew and prospered as the small, individual house churches stretched outward to share their experience of Jesus' life and love with other house churches. They understood that Christian community required a partnership of equals. "We know from Paul's letters dealing with the collection for the starving saints in Jerusalem (Rom. 15:22-27) that receiving the collection from the Gentiles was a sign of the equality of Jews and Gentiles in the partnership of the Christian community. If the Jews had refused to receive the gift from the Gentiles, they would have rejected partnership" (Rademacher, 170).

In Latin America where they do have a parish structure, albeit different in style from those found in the United States, there are great gatherings of the basic ecclesial communities (BECs) that are national and even international in scope. At these gatherings the members of the basic ecclesial communities are able to articulate their joys and struggles, to learn from and be challenged by other communities to grow in the life of Jesus. The following examples are taken from the Latin American church as recounted in *The Church from the Roots: Basic Ecclesial Communities* (55).

Many have the custom of visiting one another even when this means walking as much as four hours or more. This custom gives the sense of belonging to a larger community and of being mutually supportive in the faith and in mission.

Many communities send greetings, messages of support, and/or financial aid to other communities and even to other countries. These greetings or messages often take the form of banners, weavings or other typical products of the region. Through these means the BECs communicate aspects of their particular experience that are most challenging and central to the problems of everyday life. Everyone in the community signs the greeting. They send it as a symbol of solidarity with other communities who are committed to the same struggle, united in faith and communion.

The BECs that make progress sooner or later feel the necessity of initiating other BECs. It is no longer a matter of just a few missionaries being sent out: in Bolivia, for instance, entire communities and groups go out together to stimulate and encourage the birth of other BECs. They recount what the experience of being in a BEC has meant, both to individual members and to the community in general. This is especially convincing, since it is the testimony of the total community.

In the United States efforts are being made within parishes, and on regional and national levels, to create networking among small Christian communities. Beginning in 1990, the University of Notre Dame has held several national and international consultations on small Christian communities. In 1999 an international consultation was held in Bolivia, orchestrated by Fr. Robert Pelton, C.S.C. and the University of Notre Dame, at which representatives from six continents reported on the experience of small Christian community in their parts of the world. In 2002 the University of Notre Dame, along with the Center for Mission Research and Study at Maryknoll, sponsored an informal study of the spirituality of small Christian communities. A directed exchange of letters between partnerships formed in 42 specifically chosen communities achieved a snapshot of small Christian communities affecting the church and wider community, and vice versa, as well as mutual awareness among communities of different cultures. The partnerships facilitated by this study include Australia and Malawi, Canada and Mexico, Chile and El Salvador, Eastern Europe and Philippines, India and Tanzania, Indonesia and Togo, Ireland and United States.

The national organization, Buena Vista, exists solely for the purpose of supporting and networking small Christian communities. In addition to its bimonthly newsletter, *Buena Vista Ink*, it holds both regional and national gatherings that bring small community members together to share their experience of connecting faith and life. The National Alliance of Parishes Restructuring into Communities is another national network that works on the local, regional and national levels to support those parishes which are making small Christian community development their main priority. The North American Forum for Small Christian Communities gathers diocesan personnel who work with SCCs. Together these three organizations have held large joint national gatherings of small Christian community members in 1993, 1997 and 2002.

In his study of small groups in American society Robert Wuthnow found that 4 in 10 Americans belong to a small group that provides caring and support for its members, and that more than half of these have a spiritual or religious orientation. While he finds that these "groups are a significant feature of what holds our society together," he worries about the shallow spirituality of so much of their activity. In his words, "The movement stands at an important crossroads in its history, a turning point requiring it to choose which of two directions it will go. It can continue on its present course. Or it can attempt to move to a higher level of interpersonal and spiritual quality. Given its success over the past two decades, it can easily maintain the same course, drawing millions of participants by making them feel good about themselves and by encouraging them to develop a domesticated, pragmatic form of spirituality. By helping people feel comfortable, it can perhaps even expand its numbers. The other option will require it to focus less on numerical success and more on the quality of its offerings. Besides comforting its members, the movement may find itself challenging them at deeper levels—to make more serious commitments to others who are in need, to serve the wider community, and to stand in worshipful, obedient awe of the sacred itself" (*Sharing the Journey*, 27).

The world is getting smaller every day as we hear the stories of small Christian community members in the parish, city, country and world. Their stories of the wonderful works of God inspire us. Their stories of the struggles of the Christian journey both affirm and challenge our own journey. Their presence *in* the world encourages us to be a presence *to* the world.

Sharing Questions

Let each person who wishes respond to the questions below before anyone speaks a second time, then let open discussion begin:

- ❍ Why connect with other SCCs?
- ❍ How do Wuthnow's findings and concerns shed light on our own SCC experience?
- ❍ How can we both spread the SCC experience and challenge for more depth in the SCC style of church in the parish? in the diocese?

Action

Plan to do one or more of the following actions either as a group at this session or individually in the coming weeks:

- ❍ Visit another small Christian community.
- ❍ Gather SCCs in your parish or city.
- ❍ Read books found in the bibliography.
- ❍ Find out more about Buena Vista (*www.buenavista.org*). If you're not already a member, consider joining the organization.

Shared Prayer

Facilitator invites group members to quiet themselves for prayer, then reads this prayer aloud:

> Loving God, we hold in prayer before you all the concerns of our hearts and our lives. As a community we now share our prayers of thankfulness and of petition.

At this time, members share intentions for the community and personal intentions.

Closing Prayer

Circles

Reader 1:

"God, who lives above the circle that is the earth... has stretched out the heavens like a cloth, spread them like a tent for humanity to live in" (Isaiah 40:22).

Reader 2:

We live on a spinning circle,
Traveling in circles around the sun,
In a solar system that circles within a galaxy,
In a galaxy that circles in a universe.
The circle, no beginning, no end,
A constant reminder of the eternity of God
Circular motion, finding the source of its energy
In the center,
A constant reminder of our own needs.
We are connected within that circle,
Dependent on one another to be complete
To present the true image of God.

All:

God of no beginning and end,
source of our strength and our motion,
help us to be connected to You and to
one another.
We ask this in the name of Jesus. *Amen.*

(adapted from *Rituals and Icebreakers: Practical Tools for Forming Community* by Kathleen O'Connell Chesto)

Session Six

TRANSFORMATION: OUR MISSION

Scripture

Facilitator asks someone who has prepared ahead to read the scripture aloud:

> Therefore if anyone is in Christ, that person is a new creation; the old has passed away and, behold, the new has come. All this is from God, who through Christ reconciled us to himself, that is, God was in Christ reconciling the world to himself, not counting their trespasses against them, and entrusting to us the message of reconciliation. So we are ambassadors for Christ, God making appeals through us on behalf of Christ: be reconciled to God.
>
> —*2 Corinthians 5:17-20*

Focus Question

In groups of two, take five minutes to prepare for the session by discussing the following:

❍ Share an experience that changed your entire outlook on life.

Commentary I

Take turns reading the following commentary aloud, with a new reader for each paragraph:

"One of the many images which early Christians used to capture the reality of salvation in Jesus was reconciliation. Christians today find that image a fruitful one because it suggests that the central experience of salvation reaches out into the many dimensions of our lives—personal, societal and even international" (Perkins, 76). The work of transformation or reconciliation, in a special way, belongs to the small Christian community. The community that hears and reflects on the word of God is brought into a process of theological reflection. Theological reflection, simply put, is bringing our lives into conversation, with scripture and Christian tradition. The more often we enter that conversation the more adept we become at theological reflection and the more open we are to God's reconciling presence in our lives and in the world.

St. Paul says that if anyone is in Christ, that person is a new creation. To be a new creation we need to be aware that God is continually calling us to newness, to new discovery of God's activity in the serene and chaotic events of life. Being reborn as a new creation is an ongoing experience. If we are to be truly open to being created and recreated by God we need to be willing to reconcile what we were so sure of with what God is trying to teach us.

And so, the task of reconciliation first begins with ourselves. How do we open ourselves so that Jesus can touch our lives, recreate our lives, reconcile our lives with God who is love? Often our perceptions, prejudices and assumptions are challenged as we listen to the stories of others in our small Christian community. What we take for granted as being obvious and indisputable may, for others, be insignificant or totally irrelevant. The temptation when confronting conflict is to argue or to terminate the relationship—this may be especially true when the focus of our dialogue is scriptural or religious truth. As we begin to realize that God works in other ways than those that we *think* we understand, we become more open to the significance of others' stories—we become a new creation.

The Jewish tradition of circumcision as a sign of covenant with God was foundational in the first Christian community at Jerusalem. A dispute arose in the early church surrounding the practice of circumcision and adherence to other religious practices found in the Jewish tradition. Did Gentiles converting to the fledgling Christian faith have to be circumcised and follow Jewish ritual law? Proponents on both sides of the question brought their concern to the first Church Council, the Council of Jerusalem. There God made of the church a new creation, a transformed church. Those early Christians realized that God came to call all the people into the kingdom, not just those who followed Jewish custom. In abandoning the ritual practice of circumcision, the young church rejected male-oriented, patriarchal requirements for membership in the Christian community. In its transformation the early church became more reconciled to God's will.

Our small Christian communities help us to be open because, as we grow in love and trust for the members of our small community, we also become more open to different opinions, different insights, different wisdom. We begin to see the glory of God reflected in the lives of our brothers and sisters. The gift of reconciling ourselves with God's activity in the world is learned and practiced within our small community and is also intended to help us transform the environments in which we live and work.

"One needs constantly to analyze and diagnose everyday reality in the light of the faith, and re-educate oneself through new life experiences, using criteria other than those of a consumer society. As one community puts it, 'It is a matter of no longer buying the shirt that we do not need with the money that we do not have.' And one needs also to join with others in making concrete and constructive steps towards solving problems, continually opening new perspectives on history and creating new opportunities...so that people at the grassroots level can articulate their needs and exercise their capacity for being actively involved in their society" (Marins, 59).

Transformation and reconciliation are ongoing work. Our small communities become the catalyst for the process, then help us to implement the changes that are called for. As a community we work together to reconcile our lives to God's will. Our community becomes a new creation that labors to proclaim the reign of God in our homes, parish, neighborhood, workplace and world.

Sharing Questions

Let each person who wishes respond to the questions below before anyone speaks a second time, then let open discussion begin:

❍ How has my life been transformed by membership in our small Christian community?

- What is the transformation that Jesus is asking of us today so that our small Christian community may truly be a community of reconciliation?
- How can small Christian communities become active agents in transforming the world?

Commentary II: A Post-September 11, 2001 Reflection

Three readers take turns reading this passage aloud:

In these first years of the twenty-first century, our notion of community continues to expand and be expanded by technology, communication, terrorism and war. The vulnerability, astonishment and lingering questions presented by the tragedy of September 11 confront our identity, theology and participation in social sin. The tasks of transformation and reconciliation intrinsic to the Christian community may seem more daunting now than ever. The issues raised by September 11 are not clear-cut; the solutions (perhaps that is not even an appropriate word) are hidden in the complexity of on-going conversation and the necessary development of mutual, respectful relationships.

The question "Who is my neighbor?" continues to haunt the followers of Jesus. Who belongs to Jesus' community? His model of inclusiveness and forgiveness remains a challenge we struggle again and again to live out in our post-modern world. Just as the first Christian community struggled to expand their understanding of God and who God's people were, we too are engaged in that same task. Simplistic answers and closed paradigms tempt us; yet they cannot reflect the Jesus who came to be for us the very love of God.

The Jesus who walks on water bids us, his disciples, to follow. The only trouble is that a water-walker leaves no footsteps in which to follow, no well-worn pathway. All we know with certainty is that the way is love. How we live out that love, at this time in history, in our diverse and complex world is the challenge and the blessing of the Christian life. Our small communities provide us with the prayerful, reflective space in which to deeply question the way of love and how it should influence our words and actions. May our questioning be courageous and our responses grounded in God's unfathomable love.

Additional Sharing Questions

- How do we answer the question, "Who is my neighbor?" today, and how do we live out the way of love that Jesus came to show us?
- How does our small community help us to answer these questions?

Action

Prepare a Reconciliation Service for your SCC. Read again about the task of reconciliation on pages 39-42. Include singing, prayer, sharing and ritual. Use the SCC booklet *Designing Ritual: Celebrating the Sacred in the Ordinary* (Living the Good News/Buena Vista) for a guide to developing community-designed prayer services.

Look back over all the action sections of the previous sessions. Ask yourselves:

- ❍ Which one did we have a lot of energy for but not enough time?
- ❍ How could we attend to that action now in a more complete way?

Shared Prayer

Facilitator invites group members to quiet themselves for prayer, then reads this prayer aloud:

> Loving God, we hold in prayer before you all the concerns of our hearts and our lives. As a community we now share our prayers of thankfulness and of petition. We pause to remember especially all those Christians who gather in small community the world over. And we remember others who are lonely today.

Closing Prayer

Questioning

Reader 1:

We are so uncertain, God.
We long for answers.
We want to be sure,
Sure that we have followed the right path,
Certain we have spoken the right words,
Studied the right chapters,
Chosen the right friends.
Help us to remember that You are mystery,
Life is mystery. Help us to live with the questions.

Reader 2:
Help us to live with the questions one day at a time.
You encourage us to ask for our needs, and so we now voice our special intentions.
Members share intentions for the community and personal intentions.

Reader 3:
We ask that you hear us, Lord, and answer our needs.
We offer these prayers in Jesus' name.

All:
Questions are starting points,
Beginnings of new journeys,
Windows to insight and deeper faith.
Help our small Christian community to be courageous in asking the questions,
And to see in them opportunities to grow in knowledge of you and your plan.
Amen.

(adapted from *Rituals and Icebreakers: Practical Tools for Forming Community* by Kathleen O'Connell Chesto)

Further Reading

Brown, Raymond E. *The Churches the Apostles Left Behind.* Ramsey, NJ: Paulist Press, 1984.

Cowan, Michael A. and Bernard J. Lee, S.M. *Conversation, Risk and Conversion: The Inner and Public Life of Small Christian Communities.* Maryknoll, NY: Orbis, 1997.

D'Antonio, William V., James D. Davidson, Dean Hoge and Katherine Meyer. *American Catholics: Gender, Generation, and Commitment.* Lanham, MD: Alta Mira Press, a division of Rowman and Littlefield, 2001.

Eichten, Peter, Michael Cowan, Bernard J. Lee, S.M. *Seeking Justice: Participating in the Public Life of Faith.* Denver, CO: Living the Good News/Buena Vista, 2003.

Hebblethwaite, Margaret. *Base Communities.* Mahwah, NJ: Paulist Press, 1994.

Lee, Bernard, J., S.M. with William V. D'Antonio. *The Catholic Experience of Small Christian Communities.* New York/ Mahwah, NJ: Paulist Press, 2000.

Marins, Jose, Teolide Maria Trevisan, and Carolee Chanona. *The Church from the Roots: Basic Ecclesial Communities.* London: CAFOD, 1989.

Pelton, Robert S., C.S.C., ed. *Small Christian Communities: Imagining Future Church.* Notre Dame, IN: Notre Dame Press, 1997.

Perkins, Pheme. *Ministering in the Pauline Churches.* Mahwah, NJ: Paulist Press, 1982.

Rademacher, William J. *Lay Ministry: A Theological, Spiritual & Pastoral Handbook.* New York: Crossroad, 1991.

Richard Rohr. *Hope Against the Darkness: The Transforming Vision of St. Francis in An Age of Anxiety.* Cincinnati, OH: St. Anthony Messenger Press, 2001.

Warren, Ronald L. *The Community in America.* Chicago: Rand McNally, 1972.

Wuthnow, Robert. *Sharing the Journey.* New York: The Free Press, 1994.

About the Authors

Barbara Howard is Coordinator of Small Church Communities at Spirit of Christ Catholic Community, Arvada, CO. Barb participated in both the National and International Consultations on Small Christian Community at Notre Dame University and was the founding National Coordinator of Buena Vista, a national network committed to developing and supporting SCCs. She is the former chairperson of the National Joint Task Force for Small Christian Community. Barb is a national speaker who has written for *Today's Parish* and contributed to *Conversation, Risk and Conversion: The Inner and Public Life of Small Christian Communities.* In 1997 she journeyed to Rome during the Synod for America to speak with bishops and Vatican officials about the experience of SCCs in the United States. She has a B.A. in Religious Studies and an M.A. in Community Service and Administration from Regis University, Denver. Barb is the mother of three and grandmother of four. She and her husband, Mike, have been members of the Oilers Small Christian Community for thirty years.

William V. D'Antonio, Ph.D., is a retired Executive Officer of the American Sociological Association, and is currently Adjunct Research Professor of Sociology at The Catholic University of America. He was the research director of the Lilly Foundation Grant that resulted in the book *The Catholic Experience of Small Christian Communities.* D'Antonio is co-author with James D. Davidson, Dean Hoge and Katherine Meyer of *American Catholics: Gender, Generation, and Commitment*, 2001, Alta Mira Press.